MW01130946

MILLIE
THE MAYOR BABY

BY
JESSICA YOUNG

ILLUSTRATIONS BY
JOE HUFFMAN

★

EDITED BY
JOY SEWING

• MOON & CLOVER •
PUBLISHING

FOR MATT AND HARPER,
WHO MAKE THE WORLD A BETTER PLACE SIMPLY BY BEING IN IT,

AND FOR ANYONE WHO HAS ROOTED FOR ME EVEN ONCE.

-JESSICA

COPYRIGHT © 2022 BY JESSICA YOUNG
ALL RIGHTS RESERVED.
FIRST PUBLISHED IN 2023 BY MOON & CLOVER PUBLISHING. NO PART OF THIS PUBLICATION MAY BE REPRODUCED, DISTRIBUTED, OR TRANSMITTED IN ANY FORM OR BY ANY MEANS, INCLUDING PHOTOCOPYING, RECORDING, OR OTHER ELECTRONIC OR MECHANICAL METHODS, WITHOUT THE PRIOR WRITTEN PERMISSION OF THE PUBLISHER, EXCEPT AS PERMITTED BY U.S. COPYRIGHT LAW. FOR PERMISSION REQUESTS, CONTACT INFO@MOONANDCLOVERPUBLISHING.COM.
THE STORY, ALL NAMES, CHARACTERS, AND INCIDENTS PORTRAYED IN THIS PRODUCTION ARE FICTITIOUS. NO IDENTIFICATION WITH ACTUAL PERSONS (LIVING OR DECEASED), PLACES, BUILDINGS, AND PRODUCTS IS INTENDED OR SHOULD BE INFERRED.
THE PUBLISHER DOES NOT HAVE ANY CONTROL OVER AND DOES NOT ASSUME ANY RESPONSIBILITY FOR AUTHOR OR THIRD-PARTY WEBSITES OR THEIR CONTENT.
ISBN: 978-1-956676-03-7

This book

belongs to:

Baby Millie was elected mayor to help run the city.

But she couldn't do it by herself.
She would need the help of many.

So, when the parties were over,
and the celebrations were through...

the mayor told her friends,
"We've got lots of work to do!"

"Let's fix all the potholes so
cars can drive safely through town."

"And let's make sure people have all sorts of ways to move around."

"Let's pick up all the trash.
There's more than you might think!"

"Can someone please test the water and make sure it's safe to drink?"

"The police and fire departments
will keep us safe every day."

"And the city's engineers will make sure the rain drains away."

"Let's invite businesses to the city so there are always fun things to do…"

"...and build lots of parks to play in – with swings, slides, and pools, too!"

Then a voice was heard
from the back of the crowd.

THINGS TO
CLEAN WAT
BETTER BUSE
CLEAN UP
PARKS

"But did you know there are other ways that you can get involved?"

"You can run for office during an election year..."

"...or lead a civic campaign,

write letters,

and even volunteer!"

"Anyone can make a difference –
because there's magic in each of you.

And with the support of a team…"

HOW YOU CAN GET STARTED HELPING YOUR CITY

SMALL ACTIONS CAN MAKE A BIG DIFFERENCE! WITH THE HELP OF AN ADULT, HERE ARE SOME THINGS YOU CAN DO TO HELP YOUR COMMUNITY.

1 DRAW A PICTURE OF WHAT YOU WOULD LIKE TO SEE
IN YOUR CITY AND SEND IT TO YOUR MAYOR.

2 PICK UP TRASH IN A PARK OR AT THE BEACH.

3 SORT RECYCLING IN YOUR HOME.

4 TAKE CARE OF CATS AND DOGS AT THE
ANIMAL SHELTER.

5 WRITE THANK-YOU NOTES TO YOUR LOCAL POLICE
AND FIRE DEPARTMENTS.

A NOTE FROM THE AUTHOR

SOME PEOPLE WILL READ THIS BOOK AND THINK I WROTE IT TO EXPLAIN LOCAL GOVERNMENT. BUT I ACTUALLY WROTE THIS BOOK TO EXPLAIN MAGIC AND HOW YOU HAVE MAGIC, TOO.

WHEN YOU PUT TRASH ON THE CURB AND IT DISAPPEARS, OR YOU TURN ON YOUR FAUCET AND WATER COMES OUT, A PARK OR STORE APPEARS ON YOUR STREET, OR A POTHOLE GETS FILLED WHILE YOU'RE SLEEPING — IT'S LIKE MAGIC. YOU DON'T HAVE TO THINK ABOUT IT. IT JUST HAPPENS. SO MANY TALENTED PEOPLE IN LOCAL GOVERNMENT PUT A LOT OF THOUGHT INTO MAKING THOSE THINGS HAPPEN. THOSE PEOPLE ARE ALSO MAGIC.

YOU'RE MAGIC, TOO. WHETHER YOU LOVE NUMBERS, WRITING, COMPUTERS, PETS, OR BUILDING THINGS, YOU CAN USE YOUR MAGIC WITH LOCAL GOVERNMENT. YOU CAN BE A LAWYER, VETERINARIAN, LIBRARIAN, TRAFFIC ENGINEER, BUDGET STRATEGIST, LANDSCAPER, SPEECH WRITER, VOLUNTEER, AND SO MUCH MORE.

YOU HAVE THE MAGIC TO MAKE YOUR COMMUNITY BETTER. TRY THINGS OUT. TAKE RISKS. BE BOLD. AND SHOW THE WORLD WHAT YOU DO WITH #MILLIETHEMAYORBABY.

-JESSICA

ABOUT THE AUTHOR

JESSICA YOUNG HAS A PASSION FOR STORYTELLING, SPENDING 15 YEARS IN NEWSROOMS ACROSS TEXAS BEFORE UTILIZING THOSE SKILLS IN LOCAL GOVERNMENT.

SHE EARNED HER BACHELOR'S DEGREE IN JOURNALISM FROM THE UNIVERSITY OF TEXAS AND A MASTER'S DEGREE IN LIBERAL ARTS FROM HARVARD UNIVERSITY.

SHE IS A WIFE TO A SPORTS JOURNALIST AND A MOM TO A BOOK-LOVING TODDLER NAMED HARPER LEE.

JESSICA WAS INSPIRED TO WRITE MILLIE THE MAYOR BABY TO SHOW WHAT IT TAKES TO OPERATE A CITY. SHE HOPES THAT THE BOOK ENCOURAGES READERS TO MAKE A DIFFERENCE IN THEIR COMMUNITIES.

Proudly published by

• MOON & CLOVER •
PUBLISHING

Printed in the USA
CPSIA information can be obtained
at www.ICGtesting.com
LVHW061930221123
764224LV00014B/655

9 781956 676037